WE LIFT THEM UP TO THE LORD

We Lift Them Up TO THE LORD

A Prayerbook *for* Catholic Grandparents

LORENE HANLEY DUQUIN

Twenty-Third Publications
977 Hartford Turnpike Unit A
Waterford, CT 06385
(860) 437-3012 or (800) 321-0411
www.twentythirdpublications.com

Cover photo: stock.adobe.com/Llian

ISBN: 978-1-62785-766-6
Printed in the U.S.A.

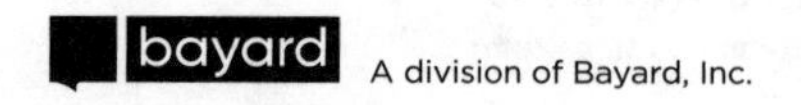

Contents

PRAYERS FOR FAMILY MILESTONES

SPECIAL PRAYERS FOR GRANDCHILDREN

Most grandparents would do anything for their grandchildren. But sometimes, because of distance, health issues, financial concerns, and family dynamics, there are limits to what actions grandparents can take.

There is one thing, however, that grandparents can do at any time and in any place. We can pray for our grandchildren. We can lift them up to the Lord. We can offer prayers for special intentions. We can thank God for giving them to us. We can ask God to shower them with love and grant them peace.

Prayers for our grandchildren may be our most powerful way to love and support them.

This is a little book of prayers for grandparents. On the first page you can write the names of the grandchildren you are lifting up in prayer. On the pages that follow, you will find prayers on a variety of topics—some of the prayers you may find helpful, while other prayers may not resonate with you. That's OK. Focus on whatever has meaning.

Perhaps the most important discovery that this little book offers is the affirmation that the Holy Spirit will guide you in your relationship with your grandchildren. The Holy Spirit will give you whatever inspiration, strength, faith, and love you and your grandchildren need. Rely on the Holy Spirit whenever you are unsure of what to say or do. Allow the Holy Spirit to work through you to touch your grandchildren in ways that are beyond anything you may have thought or imagined on your own.

My Grandchildren

My Grandchildren

Prayers for Help

IN GRANDPARENTING

Listening

Lord, help me to listen to my grandchildren with my mind, my heart, and my soul. Keep my thoughts from drifting as they speak. Let me focus on every word they utter. Help me to hear the subtle nuances beneath the surface of our conversations. Allow me to grasp the real meaning of what they are trying to say. Keep me from interrupting their stream of thought. If the situation requires that I say something, give me the words that will affirm, comfort, or support them. Never let me forget that listening is one of the greatest gifts I can give to my grandchildren. It is a sign of respect and an act of love. Lord, help me to be a good listener. AMEN.

Nurturing Gifts and Talents

Lord and Giver of Life, allow me to recognize the unique gifts and talents you have bestowed on each of my grandchildren. Instill in me the words I need to help them see that they can use their gifts and talents to give meaning to their own lives and to make the world a better place. Help me to explain to my grandchildren that everyone has a mix of strengths and weaknesses. Allow them to see that their God-given gifts offset someone else's weaknesses, and other people's gifts offset whatever weaknesses they have. Instill in them the importance of using their gifts to work together with others. Give them the courage to use their gifts and talents in ways that are pleasing to you. AMEN.

Offering Advice

Come, Holy Spirit, give me the insight to know when to offer advice to my grandchildren and when to remain silent. If a grandchild clearly needs direction but does not ask for advice, help me to discern the best way to shed light on the situation. If a grandchild asks for advice, help me to frame my words in ways that are non-judgmental, non-threatening, and filled with genuine concern. Help my grandchild see that I care deeply about whatever is happening. Give me wisdom. Give me understanding. Allow your unconditional love to flow through me to my grandchild. AMEN.

Giving Comfort

Loving and Merciful Lord, help me to comfort my grandchildren. Allow them to see me as someone who is open to hearing their strongest feelings, their agonizing questions, and their deepest fears. Instill in me soothing words of consolation. Help them to understand that as much as I would like to, I cannot take away their pain. But I can walk with them through this difficult time. Shower your love and mercy on us all. Instill in us a sense of hope that this painful period will end and that our lives will begin to move in a new direction. AMEN.

Sharing Faith

Lord God, help me to share my faith with my grandchildren—not so much in what I say but in the way I live my life. Allow me to create opportunities for them to see me pray, to attend Mass, to reach out to those in need, and to be part of a parish community. Help them to recognize the way I rely on my faith to sustain me during challenging times. Give me answers when they ask questions about faith, and give me the courage to share my faith journey with them. Let me be one of the faith-filled people in their lives upon whom they can always rely. Allow your Holy Spirit to work through me so they can come to know, love, and serve you in their own lives. AMEN.

Prayers of Petition

FOR GRANDCHILDREN

PRAYER FOR
Thriving at School

God of all Knowledge and Truth,
help my grandchildren to thrive at school. Instill in them a love of learning and the motivation to work hard at their studies. Allow them to expand their minds, to grow in knowledge, and to achieve a deep sense of understanding. Help them to discern what is good and what is true. Encourage them to use their unique gifts in ways that are pleasing to you. Bless their teachers, administrators, and school staff members. Bless the other students in their school. Make their school a place of inspiration, encouragement, and kindness. Help my grandchildren to become the kind of people you want them to be. AMEN.

PRAYER FOR FLOURISHING IN

Extracurricular Activities

Gracious and loving God, help my grandchildren to flourish in their extracurricular activities. Allow them to recognize that these activities provide an opportunity for them to expand their knowledge and to hone the gifts and talents you have given them. Instill in them the motivation they need to persevere. Keep them open to the inspirations of your Holy Spirit. Give them a deep sense of gratitude for all of the good opportunities that have been offered to them. AMEN.

PRAYER FOR

Good Sportsmanship

Come, Holy Spirit, and instill in my grandchildren an understanding of good sportsmanship on the playing field, in practices, and in the locker room. Help them to work together as a team and form good friendships with their teammates. Instill in them respect for members of the opposing team. Create in them an awareness of the need to be courteous in their dealings with coaches and officials. Help them to be gracious at all times—whether they win or lose. Allow them to see that their athletic ability is a gift from you. Fill them with a deep sense of gratitude for the opportunity to participate in a sport. AMEN.

PRAYER FOR

My Grandchildren's Friends

Lord God, shower your blessings on the friends of my grandchildren. Help them to be a good influence in each other's lives. Instill in them a sense of kindness, honesty, empathy, and loyalty. Let them be a source of support in good times and in bad. When disagreements arise, give them the understanding they need to resolve their differences peacefully. Enable them to forgive each other and to seek forgiveness when they hurt one another. Allow them to recognize that your love for each of them is the anchor that holds their friendship together. AMEN.

The Gift of Faith

Lord of all creation, instill in my grandchildren the gift of faith. Help them to grow in faith. Fortify their trust in you. Let the strength of their faith banish any doubts or fears they might have. Let them see with the eyes of their souls that their faith will carry them through whatever challenges they face in their lives. Give them the courage to share their faith with others. Help them to make faith one of the pillars upon which they build their lives. AMEN.

PROTECTION FROM

Temptation

Lord Jesus, I humbly implore you to protect my grandchildren from temptation. Help them to recognize when they are being tempted and give them the strength to reject whatever is leading them astray. Allow them to see that one of the best ways to resist temptation is to talk about whatever is happening to someone they respect. Give them the courage to heed whatever good advice that person has to offer. If it is your holy will, let me be a trusted person for my grandchildren. Give me the wisdom and the understanding to help them whenever temptations arise. AMEN.

THE GIFT OF

Gratitude

Gracious and loving Lord,
one of the most profound gifts that I ask for my grandchildren is a deep sense of gratitude. Instill in them an overwhelming respect for life. Open their eyes to acts of kindness from other people. Give them an appreciation for the little miracles that happen all around them. Keep them from taking the good things in their lives for granted. Let gratitude become the foundation for the way in which they live and interact with other people. AMEN.

THE GIFT OF

Courage

Lord Jesus, throughout the Gospels, you show us by example the real meaning of courage. Help my grandchildren to be courageous in standing up for what is right and just, in speaking the truth, in helping the sick, in lifting up the downtrodden, in reaching out to the scorned and rejected. Allow my grandchildren to see that they will always have a choice to act with courage or to walk away and do nothing. Shower them with the graces they need to choose courage. AMEN.

THE REAL MEANING OF

Hope

Lord, help me to teach my grandchildren that it is OK to hope for good things in life. It is OK to hope that they will be able to use their gifts and talents in meaningful ways. It is OK to hope for good health. It is OK to hope that good things will happen in the future. But help me to show them that the real foundation for hope lies in knowing and believing that they are loved by you. Allow them to see that no matter what happens in their lives, they can have hope in the future—not because of anything they do but because of your infinite love and mercy that remain with them in good times and in bad times. Make my grandchildren people of authentic hope. Enable them to see that all good things in life come from you. AMEN.

THE SOURCE OF

Real Joy

Lord of love and joy, help me to teach my grandchildren that happiness is fleeting, but real joy lies in the depths of themselves. Give me the words to explain that joy comes from the indwelling of your Holy Spirit in their souls. Let them grow in the understanding that real joy is a feeling of inner peace that will sustain them even when things are not going well in their lives. Help me to find examples from my own life when I felt worried, sad, or stressed but was able to reach down into the depths of myself to find the serenity and peace that come from knowing that you are with me always. Be with my grandchildren always. Enable them to recognize your presence. Let them experience the real joy that rests in you. AMEN.

THE REAL MEANING OF

Love

Lord Jesus, help me to teach my grandchildren the real meaning of love. Give me the words to help them understand the deep, unconditional, *agape* love that comes from you. Help me to explain that *agape* love is the kind of love we find in the Gospels when we choose to love God, love our neighbor, forgive those who hurt us, and love our enemies. Give my grandchildren the profound understanding that *agape* love is self-sacrificing, with no trace of selfishness or desire for gratification. Let them learn the real meaning of love by experiencing your unconditional love for them. Allow your powerful love to flow through me to touch their lives. AMEN.

THE NEED FOR

Forgiveness

Merciful God, help my grandchildren to understand the need for forgiveness in their lives. Allow them to see that holding onto grudges, anger, and resentment is like pouring poison into their souls. Help them to forgive those who have hurt them. Give them the humility they need to seek forgiveness when they have hurt someone else. Help them to forgive themselves for mistakes they have made. Give me the words to explain to them the power of forgiveness in my own life and the consequences suffered by family members who refused to forgive. Make me an instrument of your merciful love. AMEN.

THE GIFT OF

Peace

Lord Jesus, you are the Prince of Peace. At the Last Supper you promised, "Peace I leave with you; my peace I give to you. Not as the world gives do I give it to you" (John 14:27). I humbly beg you, Lord, to bestow your gift of peace on my grandchildren. Allow your gift of peace to penetrate their lives and protect them from fear and anxiety. Let your peace sustain them. Let your peace flow through them to touch the lives of other people. Let them become people of peace throughout their lives. AMEN.

PRAYERS FOR Family Milestones

PRAYER FOR A

Newborn Grandchild

Thank you, Lord, for the gift of new life in our family. Bless this child with health in mind and body. Allow this tiny baby to grow in faith, hope, and love. Bless the parents. Give them the knowledge, understanding, and wisdom they need to raise this little one to adulthood. Help each member of our family to surround this child with unconditional love. Allow our extended family members—aunts, uncles, cousins—to recognize the profound gift that new life brings and the role they play in helping to support and nurture this child. AMEN.

PRAYER FOR AN

Adopted Grandchild

Thank you, Lord, for the gift of our adopted grandchild. Knit this child into the fabric of our family members' lives. Open our hearts to embrace this child with unconditional and everlasting love. Help us to nurture this child in faith. Allow us to recognize their special gifts and talents. Help us to appreciate the unique contribution that this child will make to our family. Fill our hearts with gratitude for the gift of this new life in our family. Let us always be mindful of the powerful way you are blessing us with this child. AMEN.

WHEN A

Grandchild Is Baptized

Thank you, Lord, for the Sacrament of Baptism, which makes my grandchild a member of the body of Christ. Thank you for giving my grandchild the opportunity to know, love, and serve you. Allow this child to mature in faith over the years by encountering you in prayer, in Scripture, in the sacraments, in other faith-filled people, and through active participation in a parish community. Help my grandchild to recognize the subtle presence of the Holy Spirit and to follow your will. May the grace of this sacrament serve as a guiding force throughout life. AMEN.

WHEN A GRANDCHILD CELEBRATES

the Sacrament of Reconciliation

FOR THE FIRST TIME

Merciful Lord, shower your healing love and forgiveness upon my grandchild in the Sacrament of Reconciliation. Allow my grandchild to understand the difference between right and wrong. Give my grandchild the ability to recognize the difference between following your will and deliberately turning away from you. Help my grandchild to express sorrow for offending you or hurting others. Strengthen the resolve of my grandchild to recognize and resist future temptations. Carry my grandchild to a deep sense of peace. AMEN.

WHEN A GRANDCHILD CELEBRATES
First Holy Communion

Lord Jesus, I am filled with joy as my grandchild receives your body, soul, mind, and divinity for the first time in the Eucharist. Allow my grandchild to feel your presence in a profound way on this special day and at every reception of the Eucharist in the future. Help my grandchild to always turn to the Eucharist as a source of spiritual nourishment and strength. May the grace of this sacrament enable my grandchild to grow closer to you, and to follow in your footsteps throughout life. AMEN.

WHEN A

Grandchild Is Confirmed

Come, Holy Spirit, fill the soul of my grandchild with your love during the Sacrament of Confirmation. Strengthen in my grandchild your gifts of wisdom, understanding, knowledge, right judgment, courage, holiness, and fear of the Lord. Let my grandchild experience a profound sense of awe in your presence. Spirit of truth, remain as a guide for my grandchild. Spirit of love, instill in my grandchild the desire to love unconditionally as you love, to forgive as you forgive, and to be merciful as you are merciful. AMEN.

WHEN A

Grandchild Graduates

Lord Jesus, help my grandchild to recognize the many ways the Holy Spirit has been present at every moment leading up to this momentous occasion—guiding, protecting, inspiring, supporting. Help my grandchild to understand that all good things in life come from you. Bless my grandchild on this special day. Keep my grandchild open to the movement of the Holy Spirit as the next stage of life unfolds. Shower my grandchild with your love. AMEN.

WHEN A

Grandchild Is Married

God of love, bless our whole family as my grandchild enters into the Sacrament of Matrimony. Bless this young couple as they begin their married life together. Allow them to recognize that you are present in their love for each other. Help them to understand that the grace of this sacrament will support them in good times and in troubled times. Give them the courage to forgive each other and to reach out for help when they face challenges and difficulties. Encourage the extended members of our family to offer the spiritual support and encouragement they will need throughout their married lives. Help them to remain true to you and to each other throughout their married lives. AMEN.

FOR A

Grandchild Looking for Work

Merciful Lord, help my grandchild to find meaningful employment that offers dignity, a just wage, the ability to grow in knowledge, and the chance to contribute to society. Allow my grandchild to recognize and use wisely the gifts and talents you have bestowed. Give my grandchild a sense of responsibility. Enable my grandchild to respect authority and to become a good worker. Let my grandchild follow your will in every aspect of life. AMEN.

PRAYER FOR A

New Beginning

All-powerful and loving Triune God, send down your Holy Spirit to guide my grandchild on this new beginning. Help my grandchild to recognize the subtle signs that you are always present. Allow my grandchild to hear your quiet whispers. Let my grandchild experience the gentle way in which you reveal your will. Create in my grandchild an awareness of your tender nudges that move us toward whatever is good, whatever is true, and whatever is holy. Give my grandchild the courage to follow wherever you lead—not just in this new beginning—but in all aspects of life. AMEN.

Special Prayers

FOR GRANDCHILDREN

PRAYER FOR A

Grandchild Who Is Sick

Lord Jesus, you healed the sick, restored sight to the blind, opened the ears of the deaf, cured lepers, allowed the mute to speak, and enabled the lame to walk again. I beg you to restore my grandchild to health and wellness. If a cure is not possible, give the members of our family the strength we need to nurture and support my grandchild. Give my grandchild the strength to persevere. Bless the medical professionals who are tending to my grandchild. Be with all of us through this challenging time. Help us to rely on faith, hope, and love as our anchor. Jesus, we trust in you. AMEN.

PRAYER FOR A

Grandchild with Special Needs

Gracious and loving God, you told your apostles to let the little children come to you. Please keep my grandchild with special needs in your loving care. Help my grandchild to overcome difficulties. Allow my grandchild to realize that special needs are not a curse or a burden but rather a challenge that leads to strength of character, courage in the face of trials, and empathy for people who are struggling with challenges in life. Let each member of our family recognize the giftedness of this child. Bless the parents. Bless each person who helps to guide and nurture this child. Instill in us a deep love and appreciation for this special child. AMEN.

PRAYER FOR

Unbaptized Grandchildren

Lord, you know how upset I am that my grandchildren have not been baptized. Help me to accept the decision of their parents, even though I may not understand it. Give me the patience to bear silently the sorrow that I feel. Guide me so that I can be a faith-filled role model for my grandchildren without uttering a word. Open the eyes of my grandchildren so they can see how your loving presence is the foundation for my life. Let them come to recognize that I carry them in the depths of my soul. If it is your holy will, I pray that the Holy Spirit will one day guide them to the waters of baptism. AMEN.

PRAYER FOR A

Grandchild Making a Difficult Decision

Come, Holy Spirit, help my grandchild who faces a difficult decision. Encourage my grandchild to turn to you for guidance. Help my grandchild to carefully gather the information needed to discern God's holy will. Enable my grandchild to seek wise counsel. Open my grandchild's eyes and ears and allow my grandchild to see and hear the truth in this situation. Give my grandchild the wisdom and the courage to make the right choice. Immerse my grandchild in the peace that comes from Christ Jesus. AMEN.

PRAYER FOR A
Grandchild Making Bad Choices

Lord, I am worried and upset because my grandchild makes bad choices in life. My grandchild appears to have chosen a path that leads away from you. I beg you to send your Holy Spirit to guide my grandchild onto a path toward what is good and holy. I realize that my grandchild has free will and can choose to do what is right or what is wrong. I pray that through your grace, someone or something will help my grandchild turn away from bad influences. I pray that my grandchild will begin to make good choices. AMEN.

PRAYER FOR A

Grandchild Struggling with Addiction

God of mercy and compassion,
you can see how addiction is eating away at the fabric of my grandchild's life. The addiction is destroying my grandchild's capacity for truth, self-discipline, compassion, and love. The addiction is affecting our whole family. Help my grandchild to seek help. Give everyone in our family the courage to admit there is a problem, turn our lives over to you, and find the support we need to weather this storm. Be with us, Lord. Guide us. Help us through this agonizing time. AMEN.

PRAYER FOR GRANDCHILDREN

Whose Parents Are Going through a Divorce

Lord God, you know the difficulties our whole family is facing with the breakup of this marriage. Help me to set aside my own devastated feelings and focus on how I can support my grandchildren during this stressful time. Remove from me any thoughts or feelings of anger, blame, and resentment toward either parent. Give me the wisdom and the strength to support my grandchildren. Instill in me the words that will console them. Help me to become a safe port for them as the family storm rages. Let my grandchildren see that my love for them will never end. AMEN.

PRAYER FOR

Grandchildren Who Are Grieving

Jesus, you know the depths of our family's sorrow at the loss of our loved one. Comfort us in our grief. Give me the words I need to explain to my grandchildren that when we die, we go to be with you in heaven, where there is no more pain or suffering. Help me to assure them that one day we will all be together again. Create opportunities for our family to pray for our loved one who has died and to ask our loved one to pray for us. Help us to share our memories. Allow us to console each other in our sadness. Shower us with your love and sustain us during this sorrowful time. AMEN.

HELP IN PREPARING GRANDCHILDREN FOR

My Own Death

Lord Jesus, during the Last Supper you spoke powerful words to prepare the apostles for your death. Give me the words I need to help my grandchildren prepare for my passing. Help me to explain to them that I will always love them, that love never dies, and that I will remain with them forever in their hearts. Help me to assure them that I will continue to pray for them, and they can continue to pray for me. Let me reinforce in them a sense of gratitude for the time we have spent together. Allow them to see that the memories we have made will remain with them always. Give me the grace I need to alleviate their fears and assure them that we will one day be together again in heaven. AMEN.

PRAYER OF GRATITUDE FOR THE

Gift of My Grandchildren

Gracious and loving God, thank you for the gift of my grandchildren. They have infused my life with new meaning and purpose. My love for them overflows into all aspects of my being. I am grateful for every moment I can spend with them. When I am away from them, I hold them in my heart. Help me to always be a source of love, comfort, and strength for them. Keep me open to the movement of the Holy Spirit in their lives. Make me an instrument of your unconditional love for them. AMEN.